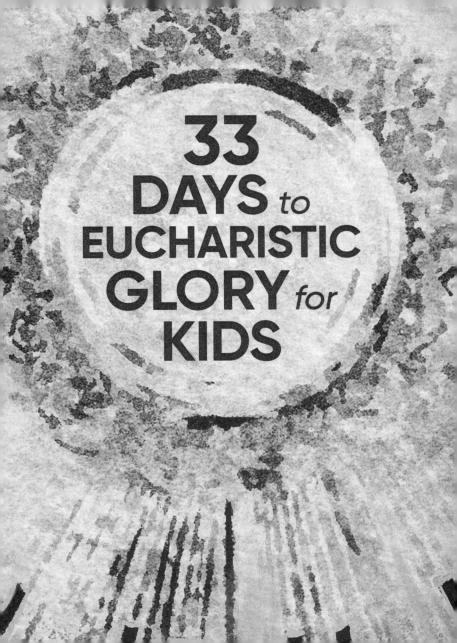

33
DAYS *to*
EUCHARISTIC
GLORY *for*
KIDS

BLUE
sparrow

Copyright © 2023
KAKADU, LLC
PUBLISHED BY BLUE SPARROW
AN IMPRINT OF VIIDENT

ISBN: 978-1-63582-544-2 (softcover)
ISBN: 978-1-63582-548-0 (eBook)
Audiobook available from Audible.

33 DAYS to EUCHARISTIC GLORY for KIDS
may be purchased for groups large and small.
For information, please call or email:
info@DynamicCatholic.com
1-859-980-7900
www.DynamicCatholic.com

International and foreign rights are available for this title.
For information, please email info@Viident.com
www.Viident.com

Designed by Todd Detering

10 9 8 7 6 5 4 3 2 1

FIRST EDITION

Printed in the United States of America

TABLE OF CONTENTS

THE FINAL DAYS: THE MOMENT OF SURRENDER

INTRODUCTION

THE EUCHARIST
is the
ANSWER

INTRODUCTION

You are about to embark on an incredible journey. This isn't just another book. It is an invitation to participate in a sacred journey—a spiritual pilgrimage. It's a guide that will lead you to encounter Jesus in the Eucharist like never before . . . and it will change your life in the most marvelous of ways.

A pilgrimage is a sacred journey with a specific intention. People travel all over the world to make pilgrimages, but you won't have to move an inch to go on this adventure. Our journey will be an inner journey, and our specific intention is consecration to Jesus in the Eucharist.

The meaning of consecration is to devote yourself to God and make yourself 100 percent available to carry out His will on this earth. It is an act of surrender to God where we hold nothing back. Through the act of consecration, we dedicate ourselves wholeheartedly to God's will, surrender our distractions and selfishness, and promise to faithfully respond to God's grace in our lives.

And there is no better way to receive God's grace than through the Eucharist. Because Jesus Christ—the King of Kings, the Lord of Lords, the Alpha and the Omega—is truly present in the Eucharist. A relationship with Jesus in the Eucharist will improve your life, strengthen your friendships, help you overcome your fears and doubts, inspire you to live the dreams God has placed in your heart, and show you the genius of Catholicism.

Jesus waits for you in the Eucharist, in our tabernacles and monstrances, and on the altar at every Mass. His message to you is unmistakable. In a world where so many people feel unseen, unheard, and unworthy, Jesus generously proclaims:

I see you.
I hear you.
I know you.
You are worthy.
I am with you.
I care.
I am yours.
You are Mine.

And this is His invitation: "Come to me, all you that are weary and are carrying heavy burdens, and I will give you rest." (Matthew 11:28)

Go to Him. Seek out time in His presence. Allow His presence to transform you in ways unimaginable.

Over the next thirty-three days I will be praying and fasting for you. I pray it will be a life-changing journey. May the Eucharistic Glory of Jesus Christ find a home deep in your soul and remain with you forever.

Are you ready for the journey of a lifetime?

HOW TO USE THIS BOOK

This book is intended as a handbook for your spiritual pilgrimage. The readings, prayers, and other resources are arranged day-by-day and under a weekly theme. This is a time of preparation for the profound experience of Eucharistic Consecration. The reflections are designed to be deeply spiritual and intensely practical.

This preparation will only take about fifteen minutes each day. Here is a step-by-step guide to each day:

1. Find a quiet place.
2. Read the reflection.
3. Ponder the one idea that struck you most from the reading for a few minutes.
4. Pray the Spiritual Communion.
5. Look for opportunities to adopt the virtue of the day in your daily activities.
6. Use the conversation starter to spark discussion with classmates, family or friends.
7. Have a great day!

The journey will last thirty-three days. Four weeks and five days. Each week is arranged around a theme and designed to prepare you for your consecration on day thirty-three, but also to educate and inspire you about the extraordinary power of the Eucharist.

Week One: The Eucharist and the Pilgrim
Week Two: The Eucharist and the Saints
Week Three: The Eucharist and You
Week Four: The Eucharist and History
The Final Days: The Moment of Surrender

If you miss a day, or two days, or even five days, do not give in to discouragement and don't quit. Discouragement doesn't come from God. If you miss days, simply read the days you missed, and keep moving forward.

Stay the course. No matter what, thirty-three days after you start: Consecrate yourself to Jesus in the Eucharist. Day 33 lays out clearly how to complete the Act of Consecration.

What you are doing is a powerful spiritual exercise that is going to bear abundant fruit in your life and for the world. Prepare for an explosion of grace in your life!

WEEK ONE

THE EUCHARIST
and the
PILGRIM

DAY 1
JUST PASSING THROUGH

"This is the day the Lord has made, let us rejoice and be glad." Psalm 118:24

For thousands of years, men and women of every age, race, and culture have sought to understand the meaning of life. You and I are no different.

Just like every other person who has ever lived, your heart longs to answer five questions:

1. Who am I?
2. Where did I come from?
3. What am I here for?
4. How do I do it?
5. Where am I going?

Our journey together will help you answer these questions. Over the next thirty-three days you will get clear about what matters most and what doesn't matter much at all. This will help you live the life God wants you to live.

The first step is facing a big truth: We are all just passing through this world. This world is not our final destination. We are pilgrims. Life is a pilgrimage. Our lives are a sacred journey toward our true home in Heaven.

Sometimes we get so busy and distracted that we forget that life is a journey. God doesn't intend for us to stay on Earth forever. He wants us to reach our sacred destination: being with Him in Heaven. That's why this thirty-three-day journey to consecrate yourself to Jesus in the Eucharist is so important. It will remind you that all of life is a sacred journey, and help you grow closer to God than ever before.

History and literature are full of epic journeys. Christopher Columbus sailed bravely across the uncharted waters of the Atlantic Ocean and discovered America. Marco Polo bridged the cultures of East and West as he traveled along the famous Silk Road in China. Odysseus took a legendary journey to get home in the *Odyssey*. Frodo and Sam persevered on their quest to destroy the Ring in *The Lord of the Rings*.

Now it's your turn.

Every year, millions of people go on pilgrimage journeys all over the world. They go to find God and connect with Him. But the truth is, you don't have to travel anywhere to go on a life-changing journey. You don't have to move an inch to connect with God. Your epic journey is a soul-adventure. And if you give it your all, it can be one of the most exciting and important experiences of your life.

Are you excited? Get ready to meet Jesus like never before!

Trust. Surrender. Believe. Receive.

LESSON

We are just passing through this world. Life is a sacred journey toward our true home with God in Heaven.

VIRTUE OF THE DAY

Patience: The virtue of patience is the ability to accept trouble, delay, or suffering without getting angry or upset. Patience makes you better at meeting life's challenges. The wisest and happiest people practice patience.

SPIRITUAL COMMUNION

Jesus,
I believe that You are truly present in the Eucharist.
I love You above all things and I want to receive
You into my soul.
Since I cannot receive You in the Eucharist at this moment,
I invite You to come and dwell in my heart.
You are the healer of my soul.
Open my eyes, my ears, my mind and my heart.
Fill me with the grace, wisdom, and courage to do
Your will in all things.
Amen.

CONVERSATION STARTER

Who is the most patient person you know? What can you learn from him/her?

DAY 2
PILGRIM OR TOURIST?

"This is the day the Lord has made, let us rejoice and be glad." Psalm 118:24

Are you going to be a pilgrim or a tourist? What's the difference? Great question.

Tourists are people who go to a new place for fun and entertainment. They get upset when things don't go as planned. Afraid of missing out, they rush around from one place to the next trying to cram everything in. They focus on themselves, often shoving past others to get where they want to go. The more you live like a tourist, the less happy you become.

Pilgrims are very different. Pilgrims are people who go on a sacred journey to connect with God. They look for signs. If things don't go as planned they ask, "What message is God trying to tell me?" Pilgrims are not concerned with seeing and doing everything, just the most important things. They are aware of the needs of others. Pilgrims count their blessings. The more you live like a pilgrim, the happier you become.

Now, let me ask you again: Do you want to be a pilgrim or a tourist? Life is a pilgrimage, but it is easy to get caught up in the things of this world and forget this truth. And that's why sometimes you need a pilgrimage to rediscover the true meaning and purpose of your life.

Remember, this planet we call Earth is not our home. We are just passing through. This life is a journey toward the sacred city, toward the heart of God, toward Eucharistic Glory, toward Heaven.

There are going to be moments in your life when you are confused and don't know what to do. The gift God gives the pilgrim is clarity. Not clarity about the rest of your life but clarity around the next step you should take. Whenever you are confused about what you should do next, remember that Jesus has all the answers. So, spend a few minutes before Jesus in the tabernacle or go to Mass and receive Jesus in the Eucharist and ask Him to show you clearly that next step.

Trust. Surrender. Believe. Receive.

LESSON

A pilgrim wakes up each day with a grateful heart and allows God to direct his or her way.

VIRTUE OF THE DAY

Joy: The virtue of joy is not the same thing as happiness. Joy lasts longer and stays around even when life becomes difficult. You can be going through a hard time and still have joy. The best way to grow in joy is to be grateful. If you want more joy, thank God for all the ways He has blessed you. The other way to grow in joy is to be kind and go out of your way to help others.

SPIRITUAL COMMUNION

Jesus,

I believe that You are truly present in the Eucharist.

I love You above all things and I want to receive You into my soul.

Since I cannot receive You in the Eucharist at this moment,

I invite You to come and dwell in my heart.

You are the healer of my soul.

Open my eyes, my ears, my mind and my heart.

Fill me with the grace, wisdom, and courage to do Your will in all things.

Amen.

CONVERSATION STARTER

What are you most grateful for today?

DAY 3
THE FOUR LAST THINGS

"This is the day the Lord has made, let us rejoice and be glad." Psalm 118:24

For hundreds of years, if you attended a retreat or a parish mission, you didn't have to wonder what the opening topic might be. You would have known. It would have been the Four Last Things. This was always the opening topic. The Four Last Things were also traditionally the topic of homilies preached on the four Sundays of Advent.

What are the Four Last Things? Death, Judgment, Heaven, and Hell. Saint Philip Neri advised, "Beginners in religion ought to exercise themselves principally in meditation on the Four Last Things." And yet, more and more, we don't reflect on these things at all, make great efforts to avoid them in conversation, and rarely hear them mentioned by spiritual teachers.

We are only here on Earth for the blink of an eye. This is not our home. That's why the happiness that God created us for is very different from the momentary pleasures of this world.

God created us for lasting happiness in this changing world and eternal joy with Him in Heaven forever. The happiness God desires for us in this life is a rare kind that doesn't depend on situations or circumstances. It is easy to be happy when everything is going well. But Christian joy allows us to be happy even when we are suffering. This is one of the key differences between Christianity and all other approaches to life.

If you look around the world, so many of the problems are caused by assigning incorrect value to people, things, and experiences. And so many of our own problems are caused by overvaluing some things and undervaluing others. We overvalue the opinions of others and undervalue the opinion of God. We focus on money and status while neglecting generosity and service.

Of all the things, people, and experiences that we undervalue, the Eucharist is at the top of the list in all three categories.

Jesus in the Eucharist yearns to fill you with His Eucharistic Glory. If you allow Him to fill you with His glory, your ability to recognize truth, beauty, and goodness will increase; you will be filled with the grace necessary to endure life's inevitable challenges and unavoidable suffering; and His Eucharistic Glory will help you reach Heaven when your journey on Earth comes to an end.

Trust. Surrender. Believe. Receive.

LESSON

Reflecting regularly on the Four Last Things—Death, Judgment, Heaven, and Hell—helps us to focus on what matters most and live life to the fullest.

VIRTUE OF THE DAY

Faith: The virtue of faith is a gift. You can work hard to develop many virtues, but with faith, we ask: "Lord, increase my faith." Ask many times each day. And as your faith grows, you will see more and more miracles, until finally, you will realize everything is a miracle.

SPIRITUAL COMMUNION

Jesus,
I believe that You are truly present in the Eucharist.
I love You above all things and I want to receive
You into my soul.
Since I cannot receive You in the Eucharist at this moment,
I invite You to come and dwell in my heart.
You are the healer of my soul.
Open my eyes, my ears, my mind and my heart.
Fill me with the grace, wisdom, and courage to do
Your will in all things.
Amen.

CONVERSATION STARTER

Discuss a time in your life when you felt close to God or full of faith.

DAY 4
THE PURPOSEFUL PILGRIM

"This is the day the Lord has made, let us rejoice and be glad." Psalm 118:24

One of my favorite phrases in the New Testament is in Luke's Gospel: "Now it happened that as the time drew near for Him to be taken up to Heaven, He resolutely turned His face towards Jerusalem." (Luke 9:51)

Jesus didn't just go, He went resolutely. To do something resolutely means to do it with determination and focus.

What do we approach with the same passion and commitment, determination and steadfastness as Jesus approached Jerusalem? Anything? Probably not. And what does that say about us?

Some people will convince themselves that they should be more committed to some worldly pursuit, whether that is getting rich, becoming famous, or achieving success. But the truth is, the reason we have not committed ourselves so fully, so totally, so completely to anything in this world, is that we are made for more. This type of commitment belongs to God and to God alone.

Jesus set off toward Jerusalem with determined resolve. It is time to bring that focus and clarity to your life.

Every encounter with Jesus in the Eucharist, whether it is at Mass on Sunday or sitting before the tabernacle for a few moments in an empty church, increases our clarity about what matters most and what doesn't matter at all. Most people are confused about what really matters, and God wants to liberate us from that confusion.

Eucharistic clarity leads us to focus on the right things. We all get to choose who and what we care about, and who and what we choose to care about determines everything. For whatever we focus on will increase in our lives.

Catholics are not called to wander aimlessly through life. There are too many people tragically wandering aimlessly through life. It is easy to get caught up in every kind of distraction. But now it is time to live with focus and take on the determination of a purposeful pilgrim.

Jesus resolutely determined to journey to Jerusalem. Let's apply that resolute determination to our earthly pilgrimage toward the Eternal City of Heaven. Are you determined?

Trust. Surrender. Believe. Receive.

LESSON
A purposeful pilgrim sets aside the distractions of this world and is resolutely determined to journey to Heaven.

VIRTUE OF THE DAY

Determination: The virtue of determination allows us to focus on a task and see it through to completion. Just keep moving in the direction of your goal or destination. Determination is taking the next step, no matter how small that step may be.

SPIRITUAL COMMUNION

Jesus,
I believe that You are truly present in the Eucharist.
I love You above all things and I want to receive
You into my soul.
Since I cannot receive You in the Eucharist at this moment,
I invite You to come and dwell in my heart.
You are the healer of my soul.
Open my eyes, my ears, my mind and my heart.
Fill me with the grace, wisdom, and courage to do
Your will in all things.
Amen.

CONVERSATION STARTER

What is something in your life that took determination to accomplish?

DAY 5
FEAR OF MISSING OUT

"This is the day the Lord has made, let us rejoice and be glad." Psalm 118:24

I had a college roommate who was constantly running from one thing to the next, staying up late, and not doing his schoolwork. One day I asked him why he was choosing this path and he said to me, "I don't want to miss out on anything during these four years." This mindset has come to be known as FOMO—Fear of Missing Out.

The idea that if we try to do everything that seems exciting and squeeze as much as possible into each day then we won't miss out is completely wrong. You are going to miss out. In fact, you are certain to miss out on most things, experiences, and opportunities.

One of the biggest traps you can fall into is the trap of FOMO. Many people make the worst decisions of their lives because they are afraid of missing out.

FOMO also has a close cousin known as "settling." The accepted "wisdom" of the vast universe known as the Internet is that you should never settle. This is horrible advice. The two most common expressions of this nonsense relate to relationships and career. "Settling" romantically means committing to someone who is less than ideal for you. The professional version of this nonsense involves "settling" for a job that pays the bills and supports your family rather than pursuing your dreams.

The truth is this: you have to settle. You don't have a choice. It is unavoidable. Our lives are finite. You do not have infinite time on this earth to pursue all possibilities. Your time is limited. You cannot become successful at anything without first settling on that path. To become a successful teacher or doctor, you set aside the possibilities of other careers and commit yourself to being a teacher or a doctor. If you bounce from one career to the next, never mastering any particular craft, you are "settling" by accepting mediocrity in many things instead of excellence in the few things that God has in mind for you.

One of the main reasons so many young people are increasingly having trouble maintaining significant romantic relationships is because they want to keep all their options open. But keeping all your options open shuts down the possibility of success in the one relationship you are in at this moment.

Every decision is a decision to miss out. Every choice for something is a choice to miss out on everything else.

Consecrating ourselves to Jesus in the Eucharist changes everything. We are no longer afraid of missing out. We know it is better to miss out on most things, because the only things that really matter are those that God has in mind just for you. Doing the will of God transforms FOMO into JOMO—the Joy of Missing Out.

Trust. Surrender. Believe. Receive.

LESSON
One of the biggest traps you can fall into is the trap of FOMO. Many people make the worst decisions of their lives because they are afraid of missing out. The only things that really matter are those that God has chosen for you. It is better to miss out on everything else. Doing the will of God transforms FOMO into JOMO—the Joy of Missing Out.

VIRTUE OF THE DAY
Discipline: The virtue of discipline allows us to maximize our contribution to the world. It teaches us to say yes to what matters most and no to what hardly matters at all. When we realize our God-given potential, our lives are filled with joy. You will never have more joy than when you live with discipline.

SPIRITUAL COMMUNION
Jesus,
I believe that You are truly present in the Eucharist.
I love You above all things and I want to receive
You into my soul.

Since I cannot receive You in the Eucharist at this moment,
I invite You to come and dwell in my heart.
You are the healer of my soul.
Open my eyes, my ears, my mind and my heart.
Fill me with the grace, wisdom, and courage to do Your will in all things.
Amen.

CONVERSATION STARTER

How would your life improve if you could make the transition from FOMO to JOMO?

DAY 6
SIX DEFINING SPIRITUAL MOMENTS

"This is the day the Lord has made, let us rejoice and be glad." Psalm 118:24

The spiritual life is chief among serious endeavors. Something that is serious is demanding and requires careful consideration and earnest application. Our need for depth and seriousness is best met with a rich inner life.

The six lessons I am about to describe to you had a seismic impact on my inner and outer life, and I am confident they will also have a great impact on your life. The definition of seismic is "of enormous proportions or effect"; I use that word very deliberately here.

The First Shift: Just Begin the Conversation. Prayer is a conversation with God. Once the conversation has begun, it can lead anywhere. Most important, it will lead to the places it needs to lead to. Never underestimate how important it is to just begin the conversation.

The Second Shift: Ask God What He Wants. When we stop asking God for what we want and start asking what He wants, we begin to open ourselves to much more than His will. We open ourselves to His wisdom. It's time for you to begin asking the Big Question: "God, what do You think I should do?"

The Third Shift: Give Yourself to Prayer. The third seismic shift occurs when we stop doing our prayer and start giving ourselves to prayer. Giving yourself to prayer means showing up and letting God do what He wants to do with you during that time of prayer. It means letting go of expectations and agendas for our time with God. It means that we trust that God is working in us no matter how we feel during prayer.

The Fourth Shift: Transform Everything into Prayer. The fourth seismic shift occurs when we discover that every activity can be transformed into prayer by offering it to God. You can try this right away. Offer an hour of homework for a friend who is sick. Offer a task you dislike for someone you know who is suffering, and do that task with great love, better than you have ever done it. Offer each task throughout your day, one at a time, to God as a prayer for a specific intention, and do so with love.

The Fifth Shift: Make Yourself Available. Do you wish to know the secret to supreme happiness? Strip away everything in your heart that makes you less available to God. The joy we experience is proportional to how available we make ourselves to God. It is through surrender that we make ourselves 100 percent available to God, allowing Him to transform us and our lives.

The Sixth Shift: Just Keep Showing Up. No matter what, just keep showing up to prayer. Keep showing up to Mass. Keep showing up for your spiritual routines. We will explore this sixth shift in more detail tomorrow, but for now, it's enough to be mindful that it's not about what we are doing. It's about what God is doing in us, through us, and with us—when we show up.

The Eucharist floods our souls with the grace needed to respond to these six seismic shifts with courage and wisdom. Each time we receive Jesus in the Eucharist, spend time in the presence of the Eucharist, or acknowledge Jesus' presence in a tabernacle, our souls flood with grace.

Consecrating yourself to Jesus in the Eucharist involves all six of these spiritual shifts. We will eventually arrive at these six significant moments in the spiritual life naturally if we stay committed to the journey. This consecration process will raise our awareness of them all over these thirty-three days.

Trust. Surrender. Believe. Receive.

LESSON
The spiritual life is not about what we are doing. It's about what God is doing in us, through us, and with us—when we surrender and make ourselves available to Him.

VIRTUE OF THE DAY

Surrender: The virtue of surrender leads to peace. If you find yourself wrestling with every situation or arguing with every person, it's time to explore why you are so insistent on imposing your will on every person and situation. The secret to surrendering to God is knowing your responsibilities and being clear about His responsibilities. Our willingness to surrender says a lot about our understanding of God.

SPIRITUAL COMMUNION

Jesus,
I believe that You are truly present in the Eucharist.
I love You above all things and I want to receive You into my soul.
Since I cannot receive You in the Eucharist at this moment,
I invite You to come and dwell in my heart.
You are the healer of my soul.
Open my eyes, my ears, my mind and my heart.
Fill me with the grace, wisdom, and courage to do Your will in all things.
Amen.

CONVERSATION STARTER

Which of the six shifts would be most helpful in your life right now?

DAY 7
THE PILGRIM'S VIRTUE

"This is the day the Lord has made, let us rejoice and be glad." Psalm 118:24

On this seventh day of our thirty-three-day journey together, I want to encourage you to persevere. Perseverance is the pilgrim's virtue. It is the ability to keep going even when things become difficult. Many people will abandon this path of consecration. Decide that you will not be one of them.

The most practical wisdom I have ever received about prayer was from an old priest many years ago, when I was a teenager and first starting to take my spiritual life seriously. The initial excitement had worn off and I was struggling to pray. Our natural and very human reaction when prayer doesn't "feel good" is to wonder what we are doing wrong. Prayer should never be judged by how it makes us feel, and we often aren't doing anything wrong. Prayer isn't about feelings.

"Just keep showing up," the old priest said to me. I didn't understand at first and when I asked him what he meant, he replied, "I'm speaking plainly. No hidden meanings, boy. Just keep showing up. Show up each day no matter how you feel or if it is convenient. Just show up and let God work on you."

This is the sixth seismic shift we mentioned

yesterday. It occurs when showing up for our daily prayer is no longer a daily decision. It becomes a commitment, a decision that no matter what you are going to show up and be with God for that time each day.

The only failure in prayer is to stop praying. You will think and feel things, and many of them don't mean what you initially think they do. So, keep showing up. Sit with whatever it is that God says to you and reveals to you. Just keep showing up.

This advice is even more relevant when it comes to the Eucharist. Some days you will be excited to go to Mass or sit before Jesus in the tabernacle. Other days it will feel difficult or like a chore. Just keep showing up either way.

Remember, it is not about what we are doing. It's about what God is doing in us, through us, and with us—when we show up. Never forget that each time you receive Jesus in the Eucharist He is working in you, to send you out into the world so that He can work through you.

Trust. Surrender. Believe. Receive.

LESSON

Just keep showing up for prayer and your other spiritual practices. Show up each day regardless of how you feel, or if it is convenient, or whether or not you think it is bearing any fruit. God's ways are mysterious. He is at work in your soul like the roots of a mighty tree beneath the surface. Just because you don't know what God is doing doesn't mean He isn't preparing you for whatever is next. Just show up and let Him work on you.

VIRTUE OF THE DAY
Perseverance: The virtue of perseverance is essential for friendship and love. It means not giving up when things become difficult. Acquiring this virtue requires both grace and significant personal effort. There is no virtue in beginning. It is easy. Many start, few finish.

SPIRITUAL COMMUNION
Jesus,
I believe that You are truly present in the Eucharist.
I love You above all things and I want to receive
You into my soul.
Since I cannot receive You in the Eucharist at this moment,
I invite You to come and dwell in my heart.
You are the healer of my soul.
Open my eyes, my ears, my mind and my heart.
Fill me with the grace, wisdom, and courage to do
Your will in all things.
Amen.

CONVERSATION STARTER
What was the highlight of the first week of your journey toward consecration?

WEEK TWO

THE EUCHARIST
and the
SAINTS

DAY 8
MOTHER TERESA: SPIRITUAL HABITS

"Set your minds on the things that are above, not on earthly things." Colossians 3:2

Mother Teresa is one of the most beloved women of all time. She emerged as an icon of goodness in the modern world. Capturing the imagination of the whole world with her heroic acts of service for "the poorest of poor," she was a steadfast voice of faith and love.

Every individual person mattered to her. "I believe in person-to-person contact," she once said, "Every person is Christ for me, and since there is only one Jesus, the person I am meeting is the one person in the world at that moment."

Those who spent time with her would often comment, "For the moment you were with her, it was as if nothing else existed to her except you."

Where did her power to love so deeply come from? What was the source of her strength to serve so selflessly? How was this woman able to inspire so many people to give their lives to God?

Here is the source: Jesus in the Eucharist. She placed Jesus at the center of her life. Eucharistic Adoration was one of Mother Teresa's primary spiritual habits. Spending time with Jesus in the Eucharist was an essential part of what made her who she was.

Mother Teresa spent the first hour of each day before the Blessed Sacrament in Adoration. Eventually, some of those close to her asked her to reduce this to thirty minutes, pointing out that every minute she spent with people had incredible impact. So, did she reduce her time? No. She increased her time of Adoration to two hours each morning and reminded those closest to her that Jesus was the source of all the fruit their work was bearing. Later, as her legend grew, she increased her daily Adoration to three hours.

Our lives change when our habits change. How would your life change if you spent an hour each day before the Eucharist? I realize that for most people this is not possible, but consider it for a moment anyway. How would your life change?

Now, consider this. What is possible? One hour a week? One hour each month? Ten minutes each day? Because whatever is possible, you should grasp it and allow the power of the Eucharist to pour into your soul.

Trust. Surrender. Believe. Receive.

LESSON

Our lives change when our habits change. Adopting the habit of Eucharistic Adoration will change every aspect of your life. We tend to become like the people we spend time with. By spending time in the presence of Jesus in the Eucharist, we become more like Him.

VIRTUE OF THE DAY

Consistency: The virtue of consistency allows us to match what we do with what we believe. It means knowing what matters most and staying true to our goal. To build consistency, pause throughout the day and make sure your words and actions are in line with what you believe to be right. Consistent people are sometimes mistaken for being boring, but the truth is they have a great peace in their lives.

SPIRITUAL COMMUNION

Jesus,
I believe that You are truly present in the Eucharist.
I love You above all things and I want to receive
You into my soul.
Since I cannot receive You in the Eucharist at this moment,
I invite You to come and dwell in my heart.
You are the healer of my soul.
Open my eyes, my ears, my mind and my heart.
Fill me with the grace, wisdom, and courage to do
Your will in all things.
Amen.

CONVERSATION STARTER

How would your life change if you spent an hour each week with Jesus in the Eucharist?

DAY 9
JOHN PAUL II: PRAYER AFTER COMMUNION

"Set your minds on the things that are above, not on earthly things." Colossians 3:2

One prayer after Communion changed my life. I was thirteen years old and Pope John Paul II was visiting Australia. My father took me to an enormous outdoor Mass. It wasn't my prayer that changed my life, it was John Paul II's prayer. His witness. His example.

When this man knelt down to pray after Communion, he would close his eyes and go to a place deep within himself. Once he was there, nothing and no one could distract him from communing with God. What does it mean to commune with God? To share your most personal thoughts and feelings with Him.

The amazing thing is, if you put that same man in a football stadium with a hundred thousand people and a million more distractions, he would still kneel down after Communion, close his eyes, and go to that place deep within himself where he connected with God. And he lived his life from that place.

You also have a place deep within yourself where you can connect with God and share your most personal thoughts and feelings with Him. How do you find the deep place within you? There is one way that I can guarantee will work. Spend time in silence. The world is a busy and noisy place, and all of that tends to distract us from what matters most. We need silence to hear God's voice in our lives.

I am not suggesting that you spend four, five, six hours a day in silence. Go to a church when it is empty and quiet. Find a quiet corner and a comfortable chair at home. Turn off your music or take out your headphones every once in a while. Have a TV-free evening once a week. Try it. It works. If you want to live from the deep place within you, visit the classroom of silence each day for a few minutes.

Find that place deep, deep within yourself, the place where you can connect with God and your truest self. Find that place, spend more and more time in that place, and begin to live your life from that deep place.

Trust. Surrender. Believe. Receive.

LESSON

Spend time in silence, so you can find that place deep within, where you are able to connect with your truest self and God. The more time you spend in silence, the more you will be able to live your life from that deep place.

VIRTUE OF THE DAY

Attentiveness: The virtue of attentiveness is found in caring for others and caring for your soul. It is an immeasurable gift from God. Attentive people notice things, inside themselves, in the situations and circumstances of daily life, and in other people. They notice the person in the room who is lonely or needs help. If you want to grow in attentiveness to God, give the person in front of you in each moment your full attention.

SPIRITUAL COMMUNION

Jesus,
I believe that You are truly present in the Eucharist.
I love You above all things and I want to receive
You into my soul.
Since I cannot receive You in the Eucharist at this moment,
I invite You to come and dwell in my heart.
You are the healer of my soul.
Open my eyes, my ears, my mind and my heart.
Fill me with the grace, wisdom, and courage to do
Your will in all things.
Amen.

CONVERSATION STARTER

What do you typically do after you receive Communion? How can you better use that time to connect with God?

DAY 10
THÉRÈSE OF LISIEUX: JESUS IN EVERY TABERNACLE

*"Set your minds on the things that are above,
not on earthly things." Colossians 3:2*

A couple of days ago we explored a little of Mother Teresa's remarkable story, but the story within the story is equally remarkable. Have you ever wondered how Mother Teresa learned to live, love, and pray the way she did?

This question leads us to another amazing Catholic woman that Mother Teresa never met. Her name was Saint Thérèse of Lisieux. Thérèse believed that love is shown through attention to the small things that fill our daily lives. Her approach to the spiritual life became known as "The Little Way."

Mother Teresa practiced "The Little Way" taught by Thérèse, and shared "The Little Way" with millions of people around the world. This connection demonstrates that every Holy Moment is a historic event. Every time we choose to love God, and collaborate with Him to love our neighbor, we change the course of human history, because our Holy Moments reverberate powerfully in the lives of people in other places and other times.

Thérèse of Lisieux entered the convent at the age of fifteen and died at age twenty-four, but her influence continues to resonate in the lives of more than 4,500 Missionaries of Charity (the order Mother Teresa founded) who work in 133 countries today. It is impossible to measure Saint Thérèse of Lisieux's impact on history, but it is vast.

Thérèse of Lisieux was a great teacher for Mother Teresa, and she will generously share her wisdom with us if we open ourselves to "The Little Way." This model of holiness is as powerful today as ever before.

I will offer you *the simplest way* I know to adopt it: Be aware of God's presence in each moment of each day. How? I will offer you the most practical way I know: At every moment, of every day, for the rest of your life, know where the nearest tabernacle is.

Where is the nearest tabernacle to your home? How close is the nearest tabernacle to your school? When you go on vacation, find out where the nearest tabernacle is. Where is Jesus? In the nearest tabernacle.

"Do you realize that Jesus is there in the tabernacle expressly for you? He burns with the desire to come into your heart." These are the words of Saint Thérèse of Lisieux.

Little things done with great love. This is what we are called to. The small things. The simple things. The practical things. It is the simple things that lead our souls to flourish.

Trust. Surrender. Believe. Receive.

LESSON

Always be mindful of God's presence in the world. Where is the nearest tabernacle? At every moment, of every day, for the rest of your life, know the answer to this question.

VIRTUE OF THE DAY

Spiritual Awareness: The virtue of spiritual awareness means being sensitive to the presence of God. It makes us mindful of how different people, things, and experiences unite us with God or draw us away from Him.

SPIRITUAL COMMUNION

Jesus,
I believe that You are truly present in the Eucharist.
I love You above all things and I want to receive
You into my soul.
Since I cannot receive You in the Eucharist at this moment,
I invite You to come and dwell in my heart.
You are the healer of my soul.
Open my eyes, my ears, my mind and my heart.
Fill me with the grace, wisdom, and courage to do
Your will in all things.
Amen.

CONVERSATION STARTER

Where's the nearest tabernacle to your home? How about to your school?

DAY 11
MAXIMILIAN KOLBE: NO LOVE WITHOUT SACRIFICE

"Set your minds on the things that are above, not on earthly things." Colossians 3:2

The history of Christianity is paved with sacrifices large and small. These sacrifices echo the love of Jesus' sacrifice on the Cross in every place and time. Self-denial and sacrificing for the sake of others is another rich theme that runs through the lives of the saints.

Maximilian Kolbe demonstrated the power of love and sacrifice during one of the darkest times in history.

Kolbe was a priest in Poland during World War II. After Germany invaded Poland he organized a temporary hospital in the monastery where he lived, with the help of a few brothers who remained. Between 1939 and 1941 they provided shelter and care for thousands of refugees who were fleeing Nazi persecution. This included hiding more than 2,000 Jewish men, women, and children from the Germans.

The center of daily life at the monastery was perpetual Adoration of the Blessed Sacrament. Kolbe recognized the evil that was growing in the world and called for constant prayer before the Eucharist.

Eventually the monastery was shut down. Kolbe was then arrested by the Nazis and sent to Auschwitz, a concentration camp. In July of 1941 a man escaped from the camp. The deputy commander picked ten men to be starved to death in an underground bunker to discourage others from trying to escape. One of the men selected cried out, "My wife! My children!" Kolbe volunteered to take his place.

After two weeks without food or water, Maximilian Kolbe was the only one alive. The guards killed him with a lethal injection so they could reuse the bunker. He died on August 14.

You and I may never find ourselves in a situation like that, but each day is filled with opportunities to take someone else's place through loving sacrifice. Each time we do, that is a Holy Moment. It is a Eucharistic moment. What small sacrifice can you make today for somebody else?

Trust. Surrender. Believe. Receive.

LESSON

There is no love without sacrifice. Love is an essential part of being a Christian, and therefore, so is sacrifice. Make small sacrifices each day that clearly demonstrate your love for God and neighbor.

VIRTUE OF THE DAY

Sacrifice: The virtue of sacrifice fills our lives with meaning. The ability to set aside our desires and personal preferences, expecting nothing in return, shows the nobility of the human person. Look for opportunities every day to do good things for others without expecting any reward and your life will be rich with meaning.

SPIRITUAL COMMUNION

Jesus,
I believe that You are truly present in the Eucharist.
I love You above all things and I want to receive
You into my soul.
Since I cannot receive You in the Eucharist at this moment,
I invite You to come and dwell in my heart.
You are the healer of my soul.
Open my eyes, my ears, my mind and my heart.
Fill me with the grace, wisdom, and courage to do
Your will in all things.
Amen.

CONVERSATION STARTER

Who has made sacrifices for you? How do you express your appreciation to those people?

DAY 12
THOMAS AQUINAS: THERE IS A DIFFERENCE

"Set your minds on the things that are above, not on earthly things." Colossians 3:2

It was a typical Wednesday morning in Naples, Italy. The year was 1273 and it was the Feast of Saint Nicholas. The burly priest was doing what he loved more than anything in the world. He was offering Mass.

The priest was known to have mystical experiences during Mass. So it wasn't that unusual that on this day, as he consecrated the bread and wine, a vision overcame him.

It wasn't the vision that shocked those who knew the priest. It was what he did next. After a lifetime of using his genius to write, the priest declared that his work was finished. When his friend asked him what had happened, he replied, "All that I have written appears to be as so much straw after the things that have been revealed to me."

Now that wouldn't mean much coming from most people, but it was a staggering statement for this particular priest. His name was Thomas Aquinas.

Over the 2,000-year history of Catholicism, Thomas Aquinas is among the greatest theologians and philosophers the Church has known. Many believe his intellectual contribution to be unmatched.

Thomas Aquinas had one of the greatest minds in human history. But he was intimately aware of an important truth that eludes many great minds.

This is the truth: There is a vast difference between knowing about God and knowing God.

Saint Thomas Aquinas wasn't just a brilliant mind. He was a man of deep prayer. And at the very center of his life was the Eucharist. It was the source of his wisdom and joy. When Thomas was in Mass, his experience of the Eucharist was often so intense that he began to tear up. Thomas had a deep relationship with God that went beyond just knowing about God. Every day he had a deeply personal encounter with Jesus in the Eucharist.

"Love takes up where knowledge leaves off," is what Thomas Aquinas observed. As we continue to deepen our relationship with the Eucharist, it is fruitful to expand our knowledge and intellectual understanding of the Eucharist. But let us never forget that it is our relationship with Jesus that animates our faith.

Trust. Surrender. Believe. Receive.

LESSON
Knowing about someone is not the same as knowing a person. Strive to know Jesus more with every passing day.

VIRTUE OF THE DAY

Wisdom: The virtue of wisdom is the good judgment to understand the outcomes and consequences of our choices on the future—in this life and in eternity. The world is drowning in information and knowledge but starving for wisdom. Wisdom is truth lived.

SPIRITUAL COMMUNION

Jesus,
I believe that You are truly present in the Eucharist.
I love You above all things and I want to receive
You into my soul.
Since I cannot receive You in the Eucharist at this moment,
I invite You to come and dwell in my heart.
You are the healer of my soul.
Open my eyes, my ears, my mind and my heart.
Fill me with the grace, wisdom, and courage to do
Your will in all things.
Amen.

CONVERSATION STARTER

Have you ever had the experience of hearing about a person, but then meeting the person and discovering he or she was completely different than what you expected?

DAY 13
SISTER FAUSTINA: DON'T DELAY

"Set your minds on the things that are above, not on earthly things." Colossians 3:2

Helena Kowalska was a nineteen-year-old Polish girl with a broken heart. She had recently given up her dream of becoming a nun and joining the convent. Her family was against it, and she did not have the financial means to enter on her own.

A few months later, on a warm summer night, something mysterious happened. Helena was at a dance with her sister. Suddenly, the music seemed to stop. The dance faded away. Helena found herself face to face with Jesus.

"How long will you keep putting me off?" He said to her. Then, just as quickly as the vision had appeared, it faded away. Helena was understandably shaken.

She believed that God had closed the door on her dream of entering the convent. But now, with this direct message from Jesus, her assumption was proven wrong.

Even though every possible obstacle seemed to be in her way, she left home and found a convent willing to open its doors to her. It was there that Helena became known as Sister Maria Faustina.

Before too long, Jesus appeared to Faustina again ...

and again . . . to share just one message: Mercy.

That message of mercy extended, in a particular way, to the Eucharist.

During one of her visions, Jesus told Sister Faustina, "When I come to a human heart in Holy Communion, my hands are full of all kinds of graces which I want to give to the soul. But souls do not even pay any attention to me; they leave me to myself and busy themselves with other things. Oh, how sad I am that souls do not recognize love! They treat me as a dead object."

A dead object. A piece of bread. A cup of wine. Dead.

When Jesus walked the earth, He made it clear that reception of His Body and Blood was not a symbolic ritual, but that in the Eucharist we indeed receive the real and True Presence of God. He reasserted this truth to Sister Faustina. He is alive, not dead. The bread is not bread, but the very life of God, sent to you out of love and mercy.

In her epic writings about Divine Mercy, Sister Faustina wrote, "You wanted to stay with us, and so you left us yourself in the Sacrament of the Altar, and you opened wide your mercy to us."

Jesus wanted to stay with us. Think about that. He wanted to stay with us. He wanted to be here with you. By consecrating yourself to the Eucharist you are becoming an agent of mercy. Beautiful, courageous, loving, transformative, never-ending—mercy.

Trust. Surrender. Believe. Receive.

LESSON

Pray and listen to what God is calling you to do. Then do it completely and without delay.

VIRTUE OF THE DAY

Mercy: Thomas Aquinas defined the virtue of mercy as "compassion in our hearts for another person's misery, a compassion which drives us to do what we can to help him." (ST II-II.30.1)

SPIRITUAL COMMUNION

Jesus,
I believe that You are truly present in the Eucharist.
I love You above all things and I want to receive
You into my soul.
Since I cannot receive You in the Eucharist at this moment,
I invite You to come and dwell in my heart.
You are the healer of my soul.
Open my eyes, my ears, my mind and my heart.
Fill me with the grace, wisdom, and courage to do
Your will in all things.
Amen.

CONVERSATION STARTER

How quickly do you respond when you feel like God is calling you to do something? Why do you resist God's call?

DAY 14
MARY: THE POWER OF YES

*"Set your minds on the things that are above,
not on earthly things." Colossians 3:2*

This consecration will help us realize how powerful our "yes" is. Free will is an extraordinary gift. It is our ability to say "yes" or "no." The ability to say "yes" carries with it an amazing power that takes a lot of reflection to truly understand. Every time you say "yes," it changes you. Forever.

Consecration is about saying "yes" to God. This Consecration to the Eucharist will be a great "yes." One of the greatest "yeses" of your life.

When the angel Gabriel came to Mary to announce that God wanted her to bear His Son, she gave a complete "yes" in response. In that moment of beautiful surrender, Mary became the first tabernacle to hold the Body and Blood of Jesus the Savior of the World. Each time we receive the Eucharist, we become living tabernacles holding Jesus too.

While there is an endless amount of inspiration to be gleaned from Mary's surrender, it is what happened next that opens our eyes to what it really means to carry Jesus into the world.

We read in the Scriptures that Mary "arose and went with all haste" to her cousin Elizabeth (Luke

1:39), who Mary had just discovered was pregnant in her old age with John the Baptist.

When was the last time you responded to your parents, teachers, or friends "with all haste"? When your mom or dad asks you to do something, or when your teacher asks you to do a little extra, do you respond with an enthusiasm to serve? We live in an age of meaninglessness because we have lost sight of the fact that our very purpose is to serve God and others. And the more we think about ourselves the unhappier we become.

Mary rushed off to serve Elizabeth. It was her first reaction. How often is your first thought for others? Too often my first reaction is one of selfishness: "I don't feel like it." "I'll do it later." "Can't someone else take care of it?" But Mary had an instinct to serve.

And still, there is another lesson here for us. The Scriptures tell us that when Mary greeted Elizabeth, the child John the Baptist leapt for joy in her womb.

How much joy do you bring to people's lives? Do people experience joy when they hear you are coming to visit? When you mindfully carry Jesus with you everywhere you go, you will become an ambassador of joy. That is what we are doing in this consecration journey. When you say "yes" to God, you will bring the joy of God to everyone you meet.

Trust. Surrender. Believe. Receive.

LESSON

Say "yes" to God in all things. Actively seek out opportunities to say "yes" to God throughout the day.

VIRTUE OF THE DAY

Humility: The virtue of humility is the starting point of the spiritual life. It means recognizing our limitations and letting God work through us. Small deeds done with humility are infinitely more pleasing to God than great deeds done out of pride. The more you know yourself, the more humility will take root in your life and soul. The life of humility is astoundingly attractive.

SPIRITUAL COMMUNION

Jesus,
I believe that You are truly present in the Eucharist.
I love You above all things and I want to receive
You into my soul.
Since I cannot receive You in the Eucharist at this
moment,
I invite You to come and dwell in my heart.
You are the healer of my soul.
Open my eyes, my ears, my mind and my heart.
Fill me with the grace, wisdom, and courage to do
Your will in all things.
Amen.

CONVERSATION STARTER
Share a time when you discovered how powerful your "yes" or your "no" can be.

WEEK THREE

THE EUCHARIST
and
YOU

DAY 15
ALL YOU WHO NEED REST

"I can do all things through Christ who strengthens me."
Philippians 4:13

There is a lot of talk these days about boundaries. It's a psychological term that refers to setting realistic limits for participation in a relationship or activity. These limits are necessary to protect the integrity of an individual or relationship.

Relationships need boundaries to remain healthy. Our lives also need boundaries to remain healthy.

God in His ever-loving providence gave us the Sabbath as the first boundary. While every other day of the week is full of all sorts of activities, we take Sunday to rest and worship God. The Sabbath is the boundary that gives us the clarity to set all other boundaries.

Rest is a divine activity. After creating the world, God rested on the seventh day (Genesis 2:2), not because He was tired, but because He knew we would get tired and need rest. God rested on the seventh day to set a boundary between the busyness of everyday life and our very human needs. God rested on the seventh day because He was teaching us that rest is essential for us to thrive.

Honoring the Sabbath sets up the boundaries we need to fully experience receiving Jesus in the

Eucharist during Sunday Mass. When we live within those boundaries and follow God's model of rest, the spiritual fruits we experience are extraordinary.

Most people are bored and tired at Mass because they are bored and tired with their lives. When we honor the Sabbath by setting Sunday aside as a special day, everything changes. From this place of rest and renewal, we will approach the Eucharist with awe and enthusiasm. Only then will we be able to comprehend what the saints have shared with us about the Eucharist, like this reflection from Padre Pio: "Every Holy Mass, heard with devotion, produces in our soul marvelous effects, abundant spiritual and material graces which we cannot fathom. It is easier for the earth to exist without the sun than without the Holy Sacrifice of the Mass!"

The Eucharist is the ultimate form of restoration, and it is best experienced when we honor the Sabbath by resting. It is time we accepted this gift that God has been trying to give to humanity since the beginning of time.

Trust. Surrender. Believe. Receive.

LESSON

Honoring the Sabbath teaches us how to set healthy boundaries in every area of our lives.

VIRTUE OF THE DAY

Rest: The virtue of rest involves taking a break from the activities of life that wear us out and grind us down, to give God a chance to fill us up and build us up. Through rest, you make space in your life for the most meaningful activities, like prayer, Mass, and time with family.

SPIRITUAL COMMUNION

Jesus,
I believe that You are truly present in the Eucharist.
I love You above all things and I want to receive
You into my soul.
Since I cannot receive You in the Eucharist at this moment,
I invite You to come and dwell in my heart.
You are the healer of my soul.
Open my eyes, my ears, my mind and my heart.
Fill me with the grace, wisdom, and courage to do
Your will in all things.
Amen.

CONVERSATION STARTER

How can you focus your Sundays to be restful and God-centered?

DAY 16
HEALER OF MY SOUL

"I can do all things through Christ who strengthens me."
Philippians 4:13

"There was a woman who had been suffering from hemorrhages for twelve years and though she had spent all she had on physicians no one could cure her. She came up behind Jesus and touched the fringe of his clothes, and immediately her hemorrhage stopped." (Luke 8:43–44)

Jesus is always healing people. Think about the Gospels. One thing we witness Him doing over and over again is healing men, women, and children.

He made the blind see, gave hearing to the deaf, cured the paralyzed, fed the hungry, comforted the afflicted, counseled the worried and anxious, forgave those burdened with guilt and shame, and even raised Lazarus from the dead.

The mistake we make is we set these stories and the people in them apart from ourselves. We don't think we need healing. But we all need healing. You may not be literally blind, but you might struggle to see your own needs and the needs of others. You may not be literally paralyzed, but you might struggle with laziness. You may not be literally deaf, but you might struggle to truly listen to God or the person in front of you. We all need healing. Jesus wants to heal you physically, emotionally, and spiritually.

Think about the story from Luke's Gospel above and connect it to the Eucharist. This poor woman had been bleeding for twelve years. Filled with faith and humility, she believed that if she could just touch Jesus' cloak she would be healed.

Here's my question: What would that woman have believed possible if she had been able to receive Jesus in the Eucharist? How do you think she would respond if she could experience the Eucharistic Glory that most Catholics take for granted every Sunday at Mass?

Now consider this. What would happen if you went to Church next Sunday looking for healing in the same way that this woman sought Jesus out to be healed? Do you believe that Jesus can heal you? Don't worry about whether He will or not for now. Just focus on believing that He can.

Trust. Surrender. Believe. Receive.

LESSON

We are blind. We are paralyzed. We are deaf. Ask Jesus in the Eucharist to heal you.

VIRTUE OF THE DAY

Trust: The virtue of trust is an acknowledgment of the reality that God is in control. It is also a belief that God has a plan for our lives and will provide for us in that plan. One of the most practical ways to grow in the virtue of trust is to become more trustworthy yourself. Trust is a key ingredient in all healthy relationships. Who we trust reveals our character. The gift of trust is a peaceful soul.

SPIRITUAL COMMUNION

Jesus,
I believe that You are truly present in the Eucharist.
I love You above all things and I want to receive
You into my soul.
Since I cannot receive You in the Eucharist at this moment,
I invite You to come and dwell in my heart.
You are the healer of my soul.
Open my eyes, my ears, my mind and my heart.
Fill me with the grace, wisdom, and courage to do
Your will in all things.
Amen.

CONVERSATION STARTER

In what area of your life do you need Jesus' strength?

DAY 17
IS SACRIFICE THE ANSWER?

"I can do all things through Christ who strengthens me."
Philippians 4:13

Love and sacrifice are inseparable.

When Jesus gave up His life on the Cross to save us, it was the ultimate act of love. This alone teaches us something about love at the foundational level. The ultimate act of love was an act of total sacrifice. Jesus held nothing back.

Every Mass is an opportunity to learn from Jesus' sacrifice on the Cross.

Each time we receive the Eucharist, we receive the Body and Blood of Jesus. Not a symbol of it. It is the same Body that He sacrificed on the Cross, the same Blood that He poured out with indescribable love. This is what Jesus is doing in the Eucharist: He is offering Himself up for you on the Cross and showing His love for you now and for all eternity.

There is no path to happiness in this life unless you can make sense of suffering, and Christianity is the only religion or philosophy that understands the transformative value of suffering. While the whole world is doing everything it can to avoid and drown out their pain and suffering, we are reminded each Sunday at Mass that our pain and suffering have tremendous value when united to the pain and suffering of Jesus on the Cross.

Sacrificial love brings meaning to our lives in a culture of meaninglessness. It binds us together in a world intent on tearing everyone apart. It provides healing in a culture overwhelmed with wounds.

There is no love without sacrifice. If you have a friendship or family relationship that is struggling, follow Jesus' model of loving sacrifice. Make sacrifices for the other person. Those sacrifices will allow more love to grow in that relationship.

We're all looking for answers in our own lives. Maybe sacrifice is the answer we have all been looking for but have refused to adopt.

Trust. Surrender. Believe. Receive.

LESSON

There is no love without sacrifice. The Cross is Jesus' ultimate teaching. It is the ultimate masterclass on love. If you have a friendship or family relationship that needs more love, follow Jesus' model. Make sacrifices for the people in your life, and the fruits of Jesus' sacrifice on the Cross will grow love in your relationships.

VIRTUE OF THE DAY

Kindness: The virtue of kindness is the ability to pour goodness into every thought, word, and action.

It allows us to bring the goodness of God into any situation. Never underestimate the value of a kind word, thought, or deed. The power of simple kindness is incredible. The future of humanity depends on the selfless caring we call kindness.

SPIRITUAL COMMUNION

Jesus,
I believe that You are truly present in the Eucharist.
I love You above all things and I want to receive
You into my soul.
Since I cannot receive You in the Eucharist at this
moment,
I invite You to come and dwell in my heart.
You are the healer of my soul.
Open my eyes, my ears, my mind and my heart.
Fill me with the grace, wisdom, and courage to do
Your will in all things.
Amen.

CONVERSATION STARTER

Who has made sacrifices for you? How is God calling you to make sacrifices?

DAY 18
THE FRUITS OF THE EUCHARIST

"I can do all things through Christ who strengthens me."
Philippians 4:13

Sometimes we need to know how something will benefit us for us to fully embrace it. And that's okay. So, let's talk about some more of the benefits of the Eucharist.

When was the last time you did something that you knew wasn't good for you? Why did you do it? Think of reasons, come up with excuses, but at the end of the day it comes down to this: You have disordered desires that are difficult to control. The grace of the Eucharist can help with that.

You aren't alone in the struggle to choose what is good for you. This happens to everyone more often than we care to admit. We know we should pray instead of watching another episode of TV . . . but there we are on the couch again. We know too much of certain types of food can make us lethargic, but we love the way they taste, so we keep eating them. We feel the tug to listen to our parents or teacher . . . but almost without thinking our phone is out and we are checking messages.

The good news is that Jesus has provided a way to conquer these situations. Not with our strength, but with His. Jesus offered His own flesh to energize our souls and give us the strength we need to turn from what is bad for us and do what is good. Each time you receive the Eucharist, Jesus gives you extraordinary gifts to help you live the life you were made for. Here is a short list of some of the fruits and gifts that flow into your soul each time you receive the Eucharist:

Friendship with Jesus.
Desire to know and do the will of God.
Cleansing of venial sin.
Hunger for virtue.
Grace to avoid sin in the future.
A heart that listens to the Holy Spirit.
Desire to know and love God.

Take a few minutes to reflect on this list. It is an incredible list of gifts. All of us need every single one of these gifts. Think about situations in your life that went wrong: Which of these gifts could have helped those situations go better? Which gift do you need right now in your life? Are you in a situation right now that would benefit from one of these gifts? Ask Jesus to flood your soul with that particular gift next time you receive the Eucharist.

Trust. Surrender. Believe. Receive.

LESSON
We all experience a struggle between what we want to do and what God calls us to do. We all have disordered

desires that need to be controlled. The grace and gifts of the Eucharist help us to navigate these struggles.

VIRTUE OF THE DAY
Receptivity: The virtue of receptivity involves opening our hearts, minds, bodies, and souls completely to God and allowing Him to work freely on our souls and in our lives.

SPIRITUAL COMMUNION
Jesus,
I believe that You are truly present in the Eucharist.
I love You above all things and I want to receive
You into my soul.
Since I cannot receive You in the Eucharist at this moment,
I invite You to come and dwell in my heart.
You are the healer of my soul.
Open my eyes, my ears, my mind and my heart.
Fill me with the grace, wisdom, and courage to do
Your will in all things.
Amen.

CONVERSATION STARTER
Which fruit of the Eucharist do you most need or desire in your life right now?

DAY 19
FIRST, LAST AND ONLY

"I can do all things through Christ who strengthens me."
Philippians 4:13

My boys love baseball and their passion for the game is contagious, so I have become fascinated with the game and all the life lessons it teaches. We recently saw a great player in his last game and I wondered what it was like for him to know he was walking out onto that field for the last time.

Think about your favorite sport and your favorite player in the history of that sport. What do you think it was like for them to play their last game? What sort of emotion do you think filled them? And what sort of longing do they still carry for the game?

These are powerful experiences and emotions, and still, it is just a game. There are things that are much more important.

There is a church in Ávila, a small city in the rolling hill country one hour northwest of Madrid in Spain. In the sacristy where the priests prepare for Mass there is a large wooden crucifix on the wall. The crucifix is surrounded by these words, which have been painted on the wall.

"Priest of Jesus Christ, celebrate this Holy Mass as if it were your first Mass, your last Mass, your only Mass."

Now, let me ask you something: How well did you participate in Mass the last time you went? If that was the only Mass you could ever go to, and the only time you could ever receive Jesus in the Eucharist, how happy would you be with the way you participated?

Imagine you could only participate in Mass one more time before God judges your life. How would you prepare for that Mass?

So, this is my challenge to you today. From now on, each time you go to Mass, participate as if it were your first Mass, your last Mass, your only Mass.

Trust. Surrender. Believe. Receive.

LESSON
Every time you go to Mass, participate as if it were your first Communion, your last Communion, your only Communion.

VIRTUE OF THE DAY
Preparedness: The virtue of preparedness means being ready, especially for death, judgment, and Heaven. Every Mass is an opportunity to grow in preparedness for Heaven.

SPIRITUAL COMMUNION

Jesus,

I believe that You are truly present in the Eucharist.

I love You above all things and I want to receive
You into my soul.

Since I cannot receive You in the Eucharist at this
moment,

I invite You to come and dwell in my heart.

You are the healer of my soul.

Open my eyes, my ears, my mind and my heart.

Fill me with the grace, wisdom, and courage to do
Your will in all things.

Amen.

CONVERSATION STARTER

How do think your favorite athlete felt (or will feel) the
last time he or she gets to play the game they love?

DAY 20
LOVE REARRANGES OUR PRIORITIES

"I can do all things through Christ who strengthens me."
Philippians 4:13

Love rearranges our priorities. Our priorities are what we give our attention, time, and effort to before everything else. They are what we care about the most. And our priorities reveal who and what we love.

When I go to Mass, something I have always noticed is that when I listen deeply to the Gospel and apply it to my life, it rearranges my priorities. Some things become less important in my life, and some things become more important. The Gospel is an invitation to love, and if we accept that invitation, our priorities will change. Love always changes our priorities.

This consecration is also an invitation to love the Eucharist more deeply, more completely, than ever before. And the result of this journey will be shifting priorities. This will look different for everyone who goes on this journey, including you. Maybe it will mean you realize Mass should come before practice for your favorite sport. Maybe it will mean you decide that it's more important to have friends who make you a better person than friends who make you popular. Maybe you'll see a shift in some other area of your life.

Many people lose friends as they grow spiritually. I don't say that to upset you, but rather to make you aware of a situation you may encounter, so you can make sense of it when it arrives. Our priorities change as we grow spiritually, and so we become less interested in doing things that don't help us to keep growing. This may include things we loved doing in the past. And if it was something we enjoyed doing with friends, it might be hard for them to understand why our interests have changed. This is an opportunity to share with them the beautiful new path you have discovered. Some people will be hungry to learn more about what you have experienced, and others will be resistant. Some people may even reject you because your mere presence challenges them to change and grow.

How are your priorities shifting as you journey through this thirty-three-day consecration? What's more important to you than it was twenty days ago? What's less important?

The Eucharistic Presence of God rearranges our priorities. Stop by an empty church sometime this week. Jesus is present there in the tabernacle. Sit with Him and allow Him to rearrange your priorities. You will never be happier than when you let God set the priorities for your life.

Trust. Surrender. Believe. Receive.

LESSON

Love rearranges our priorities. We are never happier than when we let God set the priorities for our lives. Our priorities reveal who and what we love.

VIRTUE OF THE DAY

Love: The virtue of love allows us to care for another even more than we care for ourselves. It is an overflow of the goodness that God places in your heart.

SPIRITUAL COMMUNION

Jesus,
I believe that You are truly present in the Eucharist.
I love You above all things and I want to receive
You into my soul.
Since I cannot receive You in the Eucharist at this moment,
I invite You to come and dwell in my heart.
You are the healer of my soul.
Open my eyes, my ears, my mind and my heart.
Fill me with the grace, wisdom, and courage to do
Your will in all things.
Amen.

CONVERSATION STARTER

How are your priorities different today than they were 3 or 5 years ago?

DAY 21
OUR DAILY BREAD

"I can do all things through Christ who strengthens me."
Philippians 4:13

What is the one thing that would change everything?

This consecration is your one thing now, but I would like to encourage you to be constantly thinking about this question in relation to your spiritual life: What is the one thing that would change everything?

Consecration to the Eucharist created a huge shift in my spiritual life. And there have been other habits that had a major impact over the years. The first was when I started stopping by church to pray for ten minutes a day each morning when I was in high school. My spiritual mentor had challenged me to do this. The second was the first time I really read the Gospels for fifteen minutes each day. The third was daily Mass.

I didn't go every day. When I was about sixteen, my spiritual mentor had challenged me to go to daily Mass one day each week, so I began attending Mass on Tuesday evenings at our parish. It was at Mass during the week that I discovered the genius of Catholicism and the beauty of the Mass. I would follow the opening prayer, the readings, and the closing prayer in my missal (the guide to the Mass). The words began to ignite a fire in my soul. It was only then that I began to see the incredible vision God has for our lives, for His Church, and for the world.

Now I would like to ask you something. Would your life be better if you went to Mass every day? I understand that it may not be possible, but still think about the question. I don't want it to make you feel bad about yourself. But don't let what you *can't* do stop you from doing what you *can* do. We need to learn to be honest about the best path, even if we cannot walk that path at this time in our lives. This honesty frees us to explore the question: What is possible?

When you ask yourself what is possible, you may discover that you can go to daily Mass one day each week. Maybe you can go with your parents, or friends. Great. Do it. Try to go on the same day each week and make it a holy ritual. As Saint Francis de Sales said, "The Lord delights in every little step you take." Take your next step, however small. Take it.

Trust. Surrender. Believe. Receive.

LESSON

Decide today to have a daily encounter with the Eucharist every day for the rest of your life. That encounter can be attending Mass, stopping by a church to pray before the tabernacle, or praying a Spiritual Communion.

VIRTUE OF THE DAY

Devotion: The virtue of devotion is the consistent and enthusiastic desire to please God in all things. It is the ability to keep showing up to the thing you're devoted to, no matter what. If someone observed your life, what would they think you are devoted to? Too many people misplace their devotion. Be careful not to misplace yours. Our devotion belongs to God. Give your devotion to Him with all the enthusiasm in your heart.

SPIRITUAL COMMUNION

Jesus,
I believe that You are truly present in the Eucharist.
I love You above all things and I want to receive
You into my soul.
Since I cannot receive You in the Eucharist at this moment,
I invite You to come and dwell in my heart.
You are the healer of my soul.
Open my eyes, my ears, my mind and my heart.
Fill me with the grace, wisdom, and courage to do
Your will in all things.
Amen.

CONVERSATION STARTER

How would going to Mass every day change your life?

WEEK FOUR

THE EUCHARIST
and
HISTORY

DAY 22
A DIFFICULT TEACHING

"Live justly, love tenderly, and walk humbly with your God." Micah 6:8

None of Jesus' teachings were as difficult to accept as His teaching on the Eucharist. More than any other teaching it was the one that His followers and critics alike struggled to get their hearts and minds around. Some of His followers even left Jesus over this teaching.

"Jesus said to them, 'Truly, truly, I say to you, unless you eat the flesh of the Son of Man and drink his blood, you have no life in you; he who eats my flesh and drinks my blood has eternal life, and I will raise him up at the last day.'" (John 6:53–54)

From the very beginning, the Eucharist has been a lightning rod, a point of contention and division. The same is true today. Regardless of what we have thought before or believe now, let us ask the Lord to open our hearts, minds, and souls to a deeper understanding of the Eucharist today, and with each passing day for the rest of our lives.

We are all hungry for something. Figuring out what we are really hungry for is one of the great spiritual quests of life.

There is, of course, the natural hunger for food. Some people are hungry for comfort; others are hungry to belong; still others for success, safety, adventure, security, or travel. To be human is to be hungry. Do you know what you are hungry for?

God speaks to us in our hunger. He uses our hunger to teach us and guide us. While we are searching far and wide in this world for something to satisfy our hunger, God is waiting to feed us the one thing that truly satisfies: Himself. God wants to feed us in the Eucharist.

Our constant physical hunger is meant to remind us of our constant spiritual hunger for God. Each time our stomach growls, that is a reminder that our soul is hungry too. Our soul doesn't literally growl, but it does send us messages like: *I want greater meaning. I have so much more to offer the world.*

The sad truth is that, for as many people who are physically hungry in the world, there are far more who are starving their souls.

But, unlike our physical hunger, this spiritual hunger does have a way to be perfectly and completely filled. In John 6:35, Jesus speaks these words, "I am the bread of life; he who comes to me shall not hunger, and he who believes in me shall never thirst." In the 2,000 years since Jesus spoke these words, they have not lost one bit of relevance or power. God wants to feed your soul. He wants to feed you perfectly with Himself.

The hunger in your soul is a good thing. Follow where it leads.

Trust. Surrender. Believe. Receive.

LESSON
Only God can satisfy your endless longing. Allow Him to take care of your needs and feed your soul with the Eucharist.

VIRTUE OF THE DAY
Courage: The virtue of courage is the ability to do what is good, right, just, and noble even when we are afraid. We need it most in the face of danger or difficulty, especially when something opposes our faith. Everything important in life requires courage.

SPIRITUAL COMMUNION
Jesus,
I believe that You are truly present in the Eucharist.
I love You above all things and I want to receive
You into my soul.
Since I cannot receive You in the Eucharist at this moment,
I invite You to come and dwell in my heart.
You are the healer of my soul.
Open my eyes, my ears, my mind and my heart.
Fill me with the grace, wisdom, and courage to do
Your will in all things.
Amen.

CONVERSATION STARTER
It required courage to follow Jesus 2000 years ago. How does it require courage to follow Jesus today?

DAY 23
THE LAST SUPPER

*"Live justly, love tenderly, and walk humbly with
your God." Micah 6:8*

If you knew you only had one night left to live, what
would you do tonight?

You'd spend every moment possible with the people
you love. You'd make peace with God. And you'd do
whatever you could to ensure your family and friends
knew beyond a shadow of a doubt how much you love
them.

The reality of death has that kind of effect. It clari-
fies. It makes our true priorities startlingly clear.

When it comes to Jesus, we have the unique case
of the most significant person to ever live, the source
of salvation for all the world, who knew exactly when
and how He was going to die. We would be foolish not
to look to the final days He spent on Earth for clarity
about what Jesus values above all else.

What did Jesus do on His final night on Earth?
The Gospels are aligned. Jesus gathered together His
closest friends for the Last Supper and instituted the
Sacrament of the Eucharist.

In the words of Saint Luke, "And he took bread, and
when he had given thanks he broke it and gave it to
them, saying, 'This is my body which is given for you.

Do this in remembrance of me.' And likewise the cup after supper, saying, 'This cup which is poured out for you is the new covenant in my blood.'" (Luke 22: 19-20)

When you know you are dying, it's not the moment to be cryptic, or mystical, or indirect. You wouldn't leave the doctor's office after a terminal diagnosis and write up your Last Will and Testament with a bunch of metaphors and symbols and then say to your family, "I hope you figure out what I really mean!" No. You would be specific and clear.

Jesus was clear. "This is my Body. Eat it." And "This is my Blood. Drink it." "Do this in remembrance of me." It's a clear and direct command. Jesus told His disciples that this was a sacred meal of His Body and Blood and that they should continue this practice after He was gone.

The next time you are at Mass, simply allow yourself to be in the presence of God. Quiet your mind. Imagine yourself close to Jesus at the Last Supper. You are there during Jesus' final hours on Earth. When the priest raises up the Host and says, "This is my Body, take and eat," let it sink in that Jesus is giving you the gift of His entire self. Will you give your entire self to Him?

Trust. Surrender. Believe. Receive.

LESSON

In His final hours on Earth, Jesus gave us the gift of the Eucharist. His Institution of the Eucharist changed everything. And the Eucharist continues to change everything—if we will but cooperate and collaborate with God.

VIRTUE OF THE DAY

Gratitude: The virtue of gratitude is simply about recognizing the good that is already yours. Practicing gratitude opens our eyes to all the blessings God has bestowed upon us. It is easy to overlook all the good in our lives and focus on what is frustrating or lacking. Thank every person who does even the smallest thing to assist you. And let your heart and mind be ever full of grateful prayers to God.

SPIRITUAL COMMUNION

Jesus,
I believe that You are truly present in the Eucharist.
I love You above all things and I want to receive
You into my soul.
Since I cannot receive You in the Eucharist at this
moment,
I invite You to come and dwell in my heart.
You are the healer of my soul.
Open my eyes, my ears, my mind and my heart.

Fill me with the grace, wisdom, and courage to do
Your will in all things.
Amen.

CONVERSATION STARTER

Talk about some of the people, things, experiences, and
places that fill you with gratitude for God.

DAY 24
THE EARLY CHRISTIANS

"Live justly, love tenderly, and walk humbly with your God." Micah 6:8

Are you and I rigorously seeking the best way to live the Christian life?

The first Christians were not perfect, but there was a real rigor among them for truth. It may not have been true of every member, but as a community they were rigorously seeking the best way to live the Christian life.

Today, amid the busyness and complexities of modern life, the great majority of Catholics are challenged merely to make it to Mass each Sunday.

Living the Gospel is difficult; it always has been, and it always will be. This is what today's Catholics have in common with the first Christians, and with Christians of every place and time.

There has never been a time when the Church was the perfect society Jesus calls for us to be. There have been moments when certain individuals and communities have celebrated Christ's vision in awe-inspiring ways. But sustaining these moments is the real challenge. Think of how easy it is for you to turn your back on the-best-version-of-yourself. Consider how difficult it is for you to choose the-best-version-of-yourself in different situations each day. Now multiply that by 1.2 billion and you will have some sense of how difficult it is for the Church to be the-best-version-of-herself for even a single moment. Every time you engage in a self-destructive behavior, the Church becomes a-lesser-version-of-herself. And every time you bravely choose to become a-better-version-of-yourself, the Church becomes a-better-version-of-herself.

Here's the good news: In every place and in every time since the Last Supper, Jesus has been present to guide you, me, and the whole Church through the Eucharist.

It is Jesus who will renew the world as we know it today. Will it happen with a blinding flash of light? I suspect not. The renewal that the Church and the world so urgently need at this moment in history will happen in this way: You and I will surrender our hearts to Jesus. We will allow Jesus to guide our words, thoughts, and actions one moment at a time. In this way, Jesus will bring renewal to our lives, our families, our schools, our parishes, our nations, our Church, and to all humanity.

Whatever the successes of the early Church, they were the fruit of their faithfulness to Jesus. Whatever the failures of the early Church, they were the result of rejecting Jesus. The same is true for you and me today.

Trust. Surrender. Believe. Receive.

LESSON

Humanity is in desperate need of God. The world is in desperate need of all the Church has to offer when it is thriving. Jesus wants to collaborate with you to renew the Church, so that together we can serve humanity in the powerful ways Jesus envisioned when He walked the earth 2000 years ago. But first, we need to surrender our hearts to Jesus.

VIRTUE OF THE DAY

Faithfulness: To be faithful means to be loyal, reliable, and trustworthy. The virtue of faithfulness is an invitation to place Jesus at the center of our lives and resist the constant temptation to place ourselves at the center of everything. When we are faithful to Jesus, we let Him guide everything we do.

SPIRITUAL COMMUNION

Jesus,
I believe that You are truly present in the Eucharist.
I love You above all things and I want to receive You into my soul.
Since I cannot receive You in the Eucharist at this moment,
I invite You to come and dwell in my heart.
You are the healer of my soul.
Open my eyes, my ears, my mind and my heart.

Fill me with the grace, wisdom, and courage to do
Your will in all things.
Amen.

CONVERSATION STARTER

Share a time in your life when you were the-best-version-of-yourself.

DAY 25
EUCHARISTIC MIRACLES

"Live justly, love tenderly, and walk humbly with your God." Micah 6:8

Once upon a time there was a priest who was plagued with doubts about whether Jesus was truly present in the Eucharist . . . until one day. After that day, he never again doubted that Jesus was truly present in the Eucharist.

This opening may make this sound like a story, but it is a true story as we will soon discover, and there are more than a hundred like it that have been recognized by the Church.

Even though the priest was filled with doubts about the Real Presence of Jesus in the Eucharist, he faithfully celebrated Mass every day in fulfillment of his vocation.

On this particular day, around the year 700, in Lanciano, Italy, this priest was celebrating Mass in a small church and as he said the Words of Consecration—"Take this, all of you, and eat of it, for this is my Body which will be given up for you"—the bread changed into living Flesh and the wine changed into Blood before his eyes.

Today, you can go to Lanciano and see the Flesh and Blood that has remained there for more than 1,300 years. The Flesh and Blood have been studied by scientists many times, and these scientists have concluded that the Flesh is real human flesh, and the Blood is real human blood.

Great faith and great doubt often go hand in hand, especially when it comes to accepting that Jesus is truly present in the Eucharist.

At times you may approach the altar and feel fully aware and completely certain that it is really Jesus you are receiving. These are graced moments, and this kind of faith is a gift. At other times, you may think to yourself, "Is this really true? Is Jesus really there in that tiny white Host?" In these moments, you certainly aren't the first person to have doubts.

The Miracle of Lanciano is just one of more than a hundred Eucharistic miracles that have been confirmed throughout the life of the Church.

Every Eucharistic miracle reveals the fact that just down the street at your local parish, each time the Mass is celebrated, the same miracle takes place.

These extraordinary reminders can help us overcome our doubts and open our hearts to the reality of Jesus' Real Presence in the Eucharist. But even more than that, if we open our hearts, these signs can deepen our awareness of the miracle of Jesus' presence all around us, not just at Mass, but in every moment of our lives.

Trust. Surrender. Believe. Receive.

LESSON

Great faith and great doubt often go hand in hand,

especially when it comes to accepting that Jesus is truly present in the Eucharist. Ask Jesus to strengthen your faith in His True Presence in the Eucharist.

VIRTUE OF THE DAY

Awe: The virtue of awe is extraordinary respect and reverence for the source of all life: God. You can increase your sense of awe by observing the beauty, goodness, and truth of God's creation. One great place to experience awe is in nature.

SPIRITUAL COMMUNION

Jesus,
I believe that You are truly present in the Eucharist.
I love You above all things and I want to receive
You into my soul.
Since I cannot receive You in the Eucharist at this
moment,
I invite You to come and dwell in my heart.
You are the healer of my soul.
Open my eyes, my ears, my mind and my heart.
Fill me with the grace, wisdom, and courage to do
Your will in all things.
Amen.

CONVERSATION STARTER

When you have doubts about your faith, who can you discuss your doubts with to help work through them?

DAY 26
YOUR FIRST COMMUNION

*"Live justly, love tenderly, and walk humbly with
your God." Micah 6:8*

Your First Communion is a historic event.

When you receive your First Communion, you step
into a 2,000 year history of men and women participat-
ing in Eucharistic Glory. You become part of an eternal community that includes angels and saints who all
come to the same table for this one meal. You receive
Jesus into your body and soul in the most intimate way
possible for the first time.

Whether you receive the Eucharist for the first time
at seven or seventy, that first time is just the beginning of the rest of your life. Every time you receive the
Eucharist from that point forward, you have the opportunity to have a powerful encounter with Jesus.

One of the greatest temptations around the Eucharist is to treat it like a regular part of our routine instead of the most significant moment of our week. And
the way to move beyond that spiritual obstacle is to begin to build anticipation. Anticipation means looking
ahead to the future and enthusiastically preparing for
what is to come. More than 50 percent of the joy in any
great adventure comes from anticipation. When you're
planning a sleepover for the weekend, getting ready

for Christmas, or looking forward to a vacation with your family, think about how much joy you experience just waiting for it to happen.

You can get just as excited about Mass by building anticipation. Here are a few ways you can build anticipation for Mass throughout the week: pray the Spiritual Communion each day, read the Sunday Gospel ahead of time, and arrive at church a few minutes early to quiet your heart, mind, body, and soul before Mass begins.

We prepare for everything we consider to be important in this life. Preparation builds anticipation. And anticipation fills our souls with joy. When we don't prepare for Mass, we miss out on so much of the joy God wants to give us. The more we prepare for Mass and build anticipation, the more joy we experience through the Eucharist.

Trust. Surrender. Believe. Receive.

LESSON

You have a place in the history of the Eucharist. You have a place in the history of the Catholic Church. You have a place at God's altar. Every invitation to receive Jesus is an amazing honor. Every encounter has the power to be life changing. Harness the power of anticipation by preparing for Mass.

VIRTUE OF THE DAY

Hope: The virtue of hope is a combination of desiring eternal life and expecting it. It is one of the three theological virtues: faith, hope, and love. Hope is a gift from God that leads us back to God. Repeat this simple prayer over and over throughout the day, "Lord, increase my hope."

SPIRITUAL COMMUNION

Jesus,
I believe that You are truly present in the Eucharist.
I love You above all things and I want to receive
You into my soul.
Since I cannot receive You in the Eucharist at this
moment,
I invite You to come and dwell in my heart.
You are the healer of my soul.
Open my eyes, my ears, my mind and my heart.
Fill me with the grace, wisdom, and courage to do
Your will in all things.
Amen.

CONVERSATION STARTER

What do you remember most about your First Communion? If you could do it again, what would you do differently?

DAY 27
OUR LADY OF FATIMA

"Live justly, love tenderly, and walk humbly with your God." Micah 6:8

The year was 1917. The world was at war. World War I was raging. Twenty million people had been killed and twenty-one million more had been wounded. And Mary came to warn people that even more terrible things were coming if humanity didn't change course.

Three Portuguese children received visions and messages from Mary. Their names were Lúcia, who was ten years old; Francisco, who was nine years old; and Jacinta, who was seven years old.

What was the message? It was an urgent call to conversion and penance. This is the simplest way to state it. The world was on a path to destruction. Mary offered a path to peace. And central to that path was restoring respect for the Eucharist.

The world didn't listen. Everything Mary predicted came to be, including World War II and entire countries abandoning Christianity. The world still isn't listening. Only 30 percent of Catholics in the United States believe Jesus is truly present in the Eucharist. The other 70 percent think it is just a symbol. Will you listen?

The last time Mary appeared at Fatima, she did something amazing to make her message unforgettable.

Mary had told the children that October 13 of 1917 would be the last apparition and promised a miracle that anyone in attendance would be able to witness. As many as 100,000 people were in the fields around Fatima that day and witnessed the Miracle of the Sun.

It was a rainy day. Witnesses reported that the dark clouds that had filled the sky for most of the day parted and the sun appeared as a spinning disc in the sky. Multicolored lights spread across the fields and the crowds. The sun, not as bright as usual, hurtled towards the earth before zig-zagging back to its normal position. Witnesses also reported that the ground, which moments earlier had been wet and muddy, was now bone dry, as were their clothes, hair, and shoes.

Even in the face of such amazing miracles, there are people who say we should not give too much attention to Mary, because it might take away from our attention to Jesus. Saint Maximilian Kolbe's insight was, "Never be afraid of loving Mary too much. You can never love her more than Jesus did."

Mary will always lead us to her Son. Mary will teach you to dedicate yourself to Jesus, she will lead you to consecrate your life to the Eucharist. She will lead you to Eucharistic Glory.

Trust. Surrender. Believe. Receive.

LESSON
We are all called to a continual conversion of the heart.

Receiving the Eucharist gives us the strength and courage needed to continually turn our lives back to God. Listen to Mary and she will always lead you to her Son.

VIRTUE OF THE DAY

Fortitude: The virtue of fortitude is strength in the face of difficulties and obstacles, and consistency in the pursuit of holiness. Fortitude calms our souls, keeps us from getting carried away in the moment, and helps us to stay focused on our duties and commitments.

SPIRITUAL COMMUNION

Jesus,
I believe that You are truly present in the Eucharist.
I love You above all things and I want to receive
You into my soul.
Since I cannot receive You in the Eucharist at this moment,
I invite You to come and dwell in my heart.
You are the healer of my soul.
Open my eyes, my ears, my mind and my heart.
Fill me with the grace, wisdom, and courage to do
Your will in all things.
Amen.

CONVERSATION STARTER

How would you like Mary to help you?

DAY 28
UNTIL THE END OF THE WORLD

"Live justly, love tenderly, and walk humbly with your God." Micah 6:8

Travel anywhere in the world and ask to be taken to the most beautiful building in the area. Most often, you will be taken to a Catholic church.

Whether you visit Saint Peter's Basilica in Rome, Saint Mary's Cathedral in Sydney, Las Lajas Sanctuary in Colombia, Saint Patrick's Cathedral in New York, or any of a thousand other incredible Catholic churches around the world, you will experience a sense of the sacred and the awe it inspires.

Why have Catholics built so many beautiful churches all over the world? I can tell you this: it's not about the art or the architecture, though they are often stunning. It's because we believe that Jesus is truly present in the Eucharist.

When Jesus was about to ascend into Heaven, He stood before His disciples and made an extraordinary promise: "I am with you always, to the end of the age." (Matthew 28:20)

At the heart of the Catholic faith is an unwavering belief that Jesus fulfills this promise through the Eucharist. Not only does He remain with us in spirit, He stays with us physically by giving His Body and

Blood in the Blessed Sacrament. The beauty of Catholic churches throughout the world is a celebration that Jesus is still with us. He is physically present in every Catholic church, inside the tabernacle.

Right now, even as you read this, Mass is being celebrated somewhere in the world and Jesus is once again making good on His promise to stay with us.

What does this mean for you and me in our day to day lives? Well, if we accept this as true, then everything changes. When we have a question about our lives, we can no longer act as if we don't know where to find the answer. We can go to the One who has all the answers. When we are facing a problem we cannot solve, we can no longer say we have to solve it by ourselves. We can bring it to Jesus. When we are feeling lonely or distant from God, we can no longer say we don't know where to find Him. We can go to Mass or sit before the tabernacle where Jesus is truly and physically present.

Jesus chooses to be with us—Body and Spirit—in every tabernacle and on every altar in every Catholic church in the world. He promised to be with us until the end of the world—and He will never break that promise. The only question left is: Will we choose to be with Him?

Trust. Surrender. Believe. Receive.

LESSON

Jesus promised to be with us until the end of the world. He keeps that promise every day by being physically present in the Eucharist in every Catholic church in the world. Whenever we have a problem or simply want to be close to God, we can go to a church and spend time with Jesus.

VIRTUE OF THE DAY
Sincerity: The virtue of sincerity involves being free from lies and never pretending to be someone we are not. It is achieved by controlling our words and actions with truth and justice. Keep your promises. If you say you will do something, do it.

SPIRITUAL COMMUNION
Jesus,
I believe that You are truly present in the Eucharist.
I love You above all things and I want to receive
You into my soul.
Since I cannot receive You in the Eucharist at this moment,
I invite You to come and dwell in my heart.
You are the healer of my soul.
Open my eyes, my ears, my mind and my heart.
Fill me with the grace, wisdom, and courage to do
Your will in all things.
Amen.

CONVERSATION STARTER
Describe a time when you kept a promise, even though it was difficult to do so.

THE FINAL DAYS

THE MOMENT
of
SURRENDER

DAY 29
CALLED TO HOLINESS

"This is the will of God, that you be holy."
1 Thessalonians 4:3

When you think about holiness, what comes to mind? Cabbage Patch Kids? Probably not. But even Cabbage Patch Kids can lead to a Holy Moment.

An elderly priest named William Holt was walking across a busy street when a photographer asked to take his picture for his blog, *Humans of New York*.

Father William agreed and the two men got talking. He had so many stories after decades of working with people.

"Do you have a favorite?" the photographer asked.

"Absolutely," Father William replied and launched straight into the story.

"One Christmas there was a ten-year-old girl from my parish and she was dying. All this girl wanted was a Cabbage Patch Doll. But they were sold out everywhere.

"Her mother told me, 'I've looked in every store.'

"That same day a family from my parish asked what I wanted for Christmas. I replied, 'One Cabbage Patch Doll, and two walkie-talkies.'

"They looked at me baffled and said, 'Are you sure, Father?'

"'Yes, I'm sure. I was a kid once too!' I explained to them.

"A few days later one Cabbage Patch Doll and two walkie-talkies arrived at the door.

"The Cabbage Patch Doll went to the little girl. Then I gave one walkie-talkie to her and the other one to her twin brother, so they could speak while she was in isolation. She was dying and yet she was filled with joy."

Now that's a story full of amazing Holy Moments!

As we begin these last few days of our journey toward consecration, I want to make sure that you are very clear about one thing: holiness is possible.

You are called to holiness and holiness is possible. God would not call you to something that you were incapable of living out. That would be reckless and cruel, and our God is not a reckless and cruel God. He is a God of mercy and compassion, a God who is careful and full of care.

Tomorrow we will learn how to collaborate with God to create Holy Moments like Father Holt did. Today, just treasure the thought that God wants us to live holy lives in the middle of this chaotic world.

Think you can't become holy? That's the kind of thought that's only possible when you take the Eucharist out of the equation. When Jesus in the Eucharist is at the center of our lives, holiness is possible in every moment.

Never take the Eucharist out of your equation. Trust. Surrender. Believe. Receive.

LESSON

Love is creative. Holiness is creative. There are an infinite number of ways to share the love of God with the people who enter our lives.

VIRTUE OF THE DAY

Enthusiasm: The virtue of enthusiasm leads us not just to love God and neighbor, but to energetically seek out opportunities to put our love into action. It is the opposite of spiritual laziness.

SPIRITUAL COMMUNION

Jesus,
I believe that You are truly present in the Eucharist.
I love You above all things and I want to receive
You into my soul.
Since I cannot receive You in the Eucharist at this moment,
I invite You to come and dwell in my heart.
You are the healer of my soul.
Open my eyes, my ears, my mind and my heart.
Fill me with the grace, wisdom, and courage to do
Your will in all things.
Amen.

CONVERSATION STARTER

How does the idea of Holy Moments help you believe that holiness is possible for you?

DAY 30
HOLY MOMENTS

"This is the will of God, that you be holy."
 1 Thessalonians 4:3

When I was fifteen years old, I had a great spiritual mentor. He encouraged me to read the Gospels. He taught me how to pray. He listened patiently to my questions.

One day, I was walking home from meeting with him, when everything we had been discussing for months came together in a single clarifying thought: *Some moments are holy, some moments are unholy, and our choices can guide a moment in either direction.*

In that moment I realized what was possible. In that moment I learned to collaborate with God and create Holy Moments. Now it's your turn.

It's time for Holy Moments to inject divine meaning and purpose into every moment of your life. Meaning is crucial to our health and happiness. We cannot thrive as human beings without it. And we cannot live a meaningful life by filling our life with trivial things and meaningless activities. Holy Moments solve the meaninglessness of our lives.

You might be asking, "What's a Holy Moment?"

A Holy Moment is a single moment in which you open yourself to God. You make yourself available to Him. You set aside personal preference and self-

interest, and for one moment you do what you prayer-
fully believe God is calling you to do.

One of the beautiful things about this idea is that
you do not need to study it for years. You are able right
now to collaborate with God and create Holy Moments.

And here's another beautiful thing. If you can collaborate with God today to create one Holy Moment,
you can create two tomorrow, and four the next day,
and eight the day after that. There is no limit to the
number of Holy Moments you can collaborate with
God to create. Holiness is possible.

Your choices have power. If someone had an incredible power and used it for evil that would be a horrible
thing. But what about if someone had an incredible
power and didn't use it for good? Don't you think there's
something tragic and wrong about that too?

That someone is you. You have an incredible power. You can choose what is good and holy or you can
choose what is unholy and destructive. Your choices
have power.

Consecrating yourself to Jesus in the Eucharist is a
good and holy choice that's meant to last a lifetime. How
can you live out this consecration for the rest of your
life? The answer is simple. One Holy Moment at a time.

Trust. Surrender. Believe. Receive.

LESSON

Some moments are holy, some moments are unholy,

and you get to decide. Fill your life with Holy Moments, one at a time.

VIRTUE OF THE DAY

Simplicity: The virtue of simplicity leads to happiness. It allows us to see clearly the difference between our deep needs and our shallow wants. Embrace simplicity by choosing the few things that matter most over the many things that hardly matter at all. Simplicity will free your heart to pursue holiness.

SPIRITUAL COMMUNION

Jesus,
I believe that You are truly present in the Eucharist.
I love You above all things and I want to receive
You into my soul.
Since I cannot receive You in the Eucharist at this moment,
I invite You to come and dwell in my heart.
You are the healer of my soul.
Open my eyes, my ears, my mind and my heart.
Fill me with the grace, wisdom, and courage to do
Your will in all things.
Amen.

CONVERSATION STARTER

Talk about a Holy Moment you created and how it made you feel.

DAY 31
THE WAY OF VIRTUE

"This is the will of God, that you be holy."
1 Thessalonians 4:3

The only way for our lives to genuinely improve is by growing in virtue. And it is our relationship with Jesus that gives us the strength, the grace, and the wisdom to grow in virtue.

What is virtue? It is "a habitual and firm disposition to do good." (CCC 1833)

No man or woman is born virtuous. Good habits do not come naturally. Virtue must be sought out and only grows by continual practice. You learn to ride a bicycle by riding a bicycle. You learn to play baseball by playing baseball. You learn to be patient by practicing patience.

You become virtuous by practicing virtue.

Virtue leads to better people, better living, better relationships, and a better world. If you want your life, your relationships and the world to improve, embrace virtue.

To grow in virtue is to improve as a human being. The greatest accomplishment in life is to become a better person today than you were yesterday. Ernest Hemingway observed, "There is nothing noble in being superior to your fellow man; true nobility is being superior to your former self."

Virtue is central to the growth of a Christian.

People tend to emulate the five people they spend the most time with. Are the five people you spend the most time with virtuous? Is Jesus one of those five people?

Jesus is virtue personified. He is honest, patient, kind, humble, courageous, compassionate, hopeful, wise, generous, gentle, resilient, loving. And whenever we act virtuously, something mysterious and amazing happens. We bring God's grace and goodness into the world.

Saint Peter Eymard observed, "The Eucharist is a divine storehouse filled with every virtue; God has placed it in the world so that everyone may draw from it." The Eucharist is like a treasure chest that holds something more precious than gold. It holds every virtue inside. So, draw from it abundantly and often. Go to Jesus in the Eucharist and ask Him to give you patience, kindness, generosity, love, and any other virtue you need.

Trust. Surrender. Believe. Receive.

LESSON

Virtue gives meaning and order to our lives and moves us beyond the restlessness found in every human heart. It is the key to human flourishing. Virtue leads to better people, better living, better relationships and a better world. The Eucharist is a divine storehouse filled with every virtue. The more time we spend with Jesus in the Eucharist, the more abundantly we can draw from that storehouse and grow in virtue.

VIRTUE OF THE DAY

Generosity: The virtue of generosity reflects God's infinite generosity. Give something away every day. It doesn't need to be a material possession or money. Give a compliment, a smile, advice, and encouragement. Express your appreciation. Catch someone doing something right and praise them for it. Be generous everywhere you go to everyone you meet. Live a life of staggering generosity.

SPIRITUAL COMMUNION

Jesus,
I believe that You are truly present in the Eucharist.
I love You above all things and I want to receive
You into my soul.
Since I cannot receive You in the Eucharist at this moment,
I invite You to come and dwell in my heart.
You are the healer of my soul.
Open my eyes, my ears, my mind and my heart.
Fill me with the grace, wisdom, and courage to do
Your will in all things.
Amen.

CONVERSATION STARTER

Which virtue would you like to be known for at the end of your life?

DAY 32
THE PRESENTATION OF JESUS

"This is the will of God, that you be holy."
1 Thessalonians 4:3

As we approach the end of our pilgrimage, let's reflect on this passage from the Gospel of Luke.

"When the time came for their purification according to the law of Moses, [Mary and Joseph] brought [Jesus] up to Jerusalem to present him to the Lord (as it is written in the law of the Lord, 'Every first-born male shall be designated as holy to the Lord'), and they offered a sacrifice according to what is stated in the law of the Lord..."

Put yourself there in the temple that day. Mary and Joseph have brought Jesus to present Him to the Lord in obedience to the Jewish law. Mary, the Mother of God, submits her child to the Law of Moses. Think about it: They are presenting God to God, and yet they are obedient to the law. If anyone was ever exempt from a law, it was Jesus, Mary, and Joseph in this moment. But they chose obedience. This is an amazing act of humility.

How often do we decide that a particular rule or law doesn't apply to us? When we ignore our parents, cheat on a test, or give into peer pressure to do something we know is wrong, what we are really saying is, "That rule doesn't apply to me." That is arrogance.

Why do we find obedience so difficult? We are allergic to the very word. It seems we are obedient only to our own desires. We are addicted to comfort and convenience. No wonder we have such a hard time surrendering in obedience to the will of God.

The word obedience comes from the Latin word *obedire*, which means "to listen deeply." Mary listened deeply. Joseph listened deeply. By listening deeply, they saw the wisdom of God's way.

With these inspirations in our hearts and minds, we turn to Jesus and pray:

Lord, give us patience, knowing that our impatience gets in the way of obedience. Give us the grace to see obedience as something that is life-giving rather than something restricting. Help us to become a little more patient each day and increase the desire for obedience in our hearts.

Inspire us to realize that Your guidance, rules, and laws lead us to flourish. With love and obedience, we present ourselves to You today just as Mary and Joseph presented Jesus.

Instruct us in all things; guide us in all things; command us in all things; we desire to be Your faithful servants.

Mary, pray for us and teach us to listen deeply to your Son.

Amen.

Are you ready? I think you are. Just as Joseph and Mary presented Jesus in the temple, tomorrow you will consecrate yourself and your life to Jesus in the Eucharist. This will be an epic moment in your life. Consecration to the Eucharist will change you in ways that you cannot even begin to understand. And so, my advice to you today is simple and practical: Tomorrow's going to be a momentous day, so get to bed early and get a good night's rest.

Trust. Surrender. Believe. Receive.

LESSON

Learn to listen deeply to the voice of God in your life. When we patiently listen for God's will, then obediently do what He calls us to do, we flourish and become who God created us to be. Try to patiently obey God's will in small moments and your soul will fill with joy. This will give you the courage to surrender to His will more with every passing day.

VIRTUE OF THE DAY

Obedience: The virtue of obedience is simply doing what God asks, even when you would prefer to do something else, or think there is a better way. It is also good to obey virtuous authorities like your parents and the Church who can help you flourish and know the truth. Obedience frees our souls and helps us peacefully accept the best path in life.

SPIRITUAL COMMUNION

Jesus,

I believe that You are truly present in the Eucharist.

I love You above all things and I want to receive

You into my soul.

Since I cannot receive You in the Eucharist at this

moment,

I invite You to come and dwell in my heart.

You are the healer of my soul.

Open my eyes, my ears, my mind and my heart.

Fill me with the grace, wisdom, and courage to do

Your will in all things.

Amen.

CONVERSATION STARTER

How would your life change if you saw obedience as
something life-giving rather than something restrictive?

DAY 33
TOTALLY YOURS

"This is the will of God, that you be holy."
1 Thessalonians 4:3

Today is the end of your journey. Congratulations! You did it. I hope you will find a way to celebrate.

Totus Tuus. This is a Latin phrase which means "totally yours." It was the motto of Pope John Paul II and signifies a radical commitment to Jesus through Mary. Today you are saying to Jesus, "I am totally Yours and everything I have is Yours."

This total self-giving is something we have witnessed at every Mass we have ever attended. In the Eucharist, Jesus gives His whole self to us completely and absolutely. And now, in this Eucharistic Consecration, we respond with love and generosity by pledging our whole selves to Jesus in the Eucharist.

This consecration is a radical act of love. It is a radical act of generosity. Deep down we all desire to make the radical and complete gift of self that you are going to make to God today.

Today you are offering your whole self to Jesus in the Eucharist. Don't hold anything back. Your consecration is a declaration before God. This is a historic moment. An epic moment in your spiritual journey.

You are joining your "yes" with Mary's "yes."

You are joining your "yes" with Joseph's "yes."

You are joining your "yes" with the "yes" of Peter and Paul.

You are joining your "yes" with the "yes" of Mother Teresa and John Paul II.

You are joining your "yes" with the "yes" of all of God's holy angels and saints.

Throughout this journey I have been speaking of Eucharistic Glory. So, you are no doubt wondering, what is Eucharistic Glory?

We pray in the Mass, "All glory and honor be yours forever and ever. Amen." It comes from the Book of Revelation. (5:13) But God wants us to share in His glory. *The Catechism of the Catholic Church* teaches us that the Eucharist is an invitation to share in the glory of Jesus. Receiving the Eucharist brings us close to Jesus' Heart. It strengthens us on the pilgrimage of life. It makes us long for eternal life. And it unites us here and now to the Church in Heaven, the Blessed Virgin Mary, and all the saints. (CCC 1419)

Every time we receive Jesus in the Eucharist, we touch Heaven, we are joined with all the angels and saints, and in that moment, we share in the glory of God. That is Eucharistic Glory.

Heaven and Earth meet in the Eucharist. It's time to discover all that you are, all that you can be, and all that you will be in Jesus Christ. It's time to embrace Eucharistic Glory.

And now, it is time to consecrate yourself to Jesus Christ in the Eucharist ...

PRAYER OF EUCHARISTIC CONSECRATION

Lord Jesus Christ,
Bread of Life,
True God and True Man,
The Alpha and the Omega,
Truly present—Body, Blood, Soul, and Divinity—in the Blessed Sacrament,
I consecrate myself to You today without reservation.

Here I am, Lord.
I come to do Your will.
Come and dwell within me.
Heal my body, focus my mind,
transform my heart,
and nourish my soul,
so that I may represent You faithfully in the many situations and circumstances of my daily life.

Lord Jesus Christ, truly present in the Eucharist,
I consecrate myself to You today without reservation.
I hold nothing back.
I surrender completely and absolutely to Your goodness.

I know the plans You have for me:
Plans for prosperity and well-being,
plans for good and not evil,
plans that give me hope and a future.

Lord Jesus Christ, truly present in the Eucharist,
I consecrate myself to You today without reservation.
I surrender my whole being to Your care.
I surrender my life, my plans, and my very self to You.
I place all that I am at Your feet.
I place all that I have at Your feet.
Take what You want to take and give what You want to
give.

Lord Jesus Christ, truly present in the Eucharist,
I consecrate myself to You today without reservation.
Transform me.
Transform my life.
I trust in the eternal genius of Your ways.
I make myself 100 percent available to You.
Lead me, encourage me, challenge me.
Show me how I can collaborate with You,
and I will do what You ask with a joyful heart.

Lord Jesus Christ, truly present in the Eucharist,
I consecrate myself to You today without reservation.
Grant me the grace, wisdom, and courage,
to live justly,

love tenderly,
and walk humbly with You, my God,
all the days of my life.

Angels and Saints,
Lead me in the ways of the pilgrim,
so that one day I too may share in Heaven.
With His blessing and by His grace,
bestow upon me your humility, generosity, and devotion,
and I implore you to carry this prayer to our
Eucharistic Lord.

Mary, Mother of Jesus,
Teach my soul how to receive your Son in the Eucharist,
and how to represent Him in this world.
Teach me the surrender and sacrifice that were
necessary to make the Eucharist possible in this
broken world.
Intercede for me and obtain the grace necessary
to allow your Son's teachings to penetrate
the darkest, coldest, hardest parts of my heart,
so that by receiving Him in the Eucharist
my heart may become ever more like
His Eucharistic Heart.

Amen.